FOO

It's A Funny
Old Game

FOOTBALL

It's A Funny Old Game

ANDREW JOHN
AND
STEPHEN BLAKE

Michael O'Mara Humour

First published in Great Britain in 2004 by
Michael O'Mara Books Limited
9 Lion Yard
Tremadoc Road
London SW4 7NQ

A CIP catalogue record for this book is available from
the British Library

ISBN 1-84317-091-4

1 3 5 7 9 10 8 6 4 2

Designed and typeset by Design 23

Printed and bound in England by Cox & Wyman Ltd,
Reading, Berks

Contents

Introduction 7

Stating the obvious 9

No pain, no gain 23

Who's counting? 27

Body parts 38

Time travel 46

Mixed-up metaphors 49

They think it's all over . . . 62

Introduction

If you were a sketch writer for a hit comedy show, you'd be struggling to come up with some of the things footballers and those who surround them say quite by accident. That's why this collection of one-liners (well, some have more than one line) is a laugh from start to finish.

We appreciate that commentators in the box and players suddenly confronted by a microphone are under pressure to say something. Sometimes the wrong thing comes out. Who can blame them? But without those slip-ups, we wouldn't have *Football: It's A Funny Old Game*.

Quotes from the commentary box even got their very own slot in the satirical magazine *Private Eye*, called 'Colemanballs'. No prizes for guessing whose name inspired that. And you'll find several quotes from the man himself in these pages, as you will from the likes of Terry Venables, David Beckham, George Best, Alan Shearer, Ian St John and many more.

Footballers and others in the game mostly put their feet in their mouths when it comes to metaphors; whether it's the FA knocking on Michael Owen's doorbell, the carrot at the end of a tunnel or the gelling period that's just started to knit.

And they're a great bunch for stating the obvious, such as the commentator who astutely pointed out that, if a team had a weakness in its defence, it was in its defence, or Glenn Hoddle's observation that you can't compare two players who are different because they're not the same. Hmm. We'd never have thought of that.

The nation's two favourite sports – soccer and cricket – are stuffed with quotable quotes: the downright funny in the case of the former, and the more cerebral, perhaps eccentric, always interesting and often amusing in the case of the latter, as you'll see in our companion volume, *Cricket: It's A Funny Old Game*.

Even works of compilation require the loving care of an editor, and we thank Helen Cumberbatch of Michael O'Mara Books for her unstinting help and guidance.

So spoil yourself. Buy both. And keep on the ball.

ANDREW JOHN AND STEPHEN BLAKE

SPRING 2004

Stating the obvious

You have to score goals to win in football, or else you'll become the victims of your own problems. Honest. Now that's pretty obvious, but you'd be surprised at how many people feel they have to tell you. There are more obvious things in this collection, too – obviously.

If history's going to repeat itself I should think we can expect the same thing again.

TERRY VENABLES

After a goalless first half, the score at half-time is nil–nil.

BRIAN MOORE

Batistuta gets most of his goals with the ball.

IAN ST JOHN

And latecomers to this game, mainly Rangers fans, are surprisingly coming in late.

CHICK YOUNG

The Brazilians aren't as good as they used to be, or as they are now.

KENNY DALGLISH

At the beginning it was a ninety-minute game, at half-time it was a forty-five-minute game, and now it's even shorter.

COMMENTATOR ON ABC TV

St Mirren have been under the rack.

CHICK MURRAY

You either win or you lose. There's no in between.

TERRY VENABLES

I'm a firm believer that if you score one goal, the other team have to score two to win.

HOWARD WILKINSON

DICKIE DAVIES: What's he going to be telling his team at half-time, Denis?

DENIS LAW: He'll be telling them that there are forty-five minutes left to play.

Ronaldo is always very close to being onside or offside.

RAY WILKINS

If there's a weakness in Chelsea's defence, it's in their defence.

COMMENTATOR ON RADIO 5 LIVE

RICHARD KEYS: Well, wasn't that the most nail-biting and dramatic finale?

ALAN SHEARER: Yeah, especially at the end.

I'll never play at Wembley again, unless I play at Wembley again.

KEVIN KEEGAN

If the goalkeeper wasn't there, it would've been a goal.

DAVE BASSETT

The teams at the bottom of the Premiership are conceding a lot of goals and that's no coincidence.

BARRY VENISON

The pace of the match is really accelerating, by which I mean it is getting faster all the time.

DAVID COLEMAN

Cleland was the victim of his own downfall.

ALAN PARRY

This game could go either way. Or it could be a draw.

PETER LORIMER

It's been seventeen years since Celtic first won this competition, and after tonight it could be eighteen.

RODDY FORSYTH

If Gabriel Amato's shot had gone in, the result could have been different.

GIOVANNI VAN BRONCKHORST

And the news from Guadalajara, where the temperature is ninety-six degrees, is that Falcao is warming up.

BRIAN MOORE

I was here at Maine Road when City lost four–nil to Wimbledon, but they could have been two–nil up after five minutes, and, if they had been, the final score might just have been different.

JIM BEGLIN

They compare Steve McManaman to Steve Heighway and he's nothing like him, but I can see why – it's because he's a bit different.

KEVIN KEEGAN

Football games turn on things that are done by players.

WILLIE MILLER

That shot might not have been as good as it might have been.

JOHN MOTSON

He was in a no-win situation, unless he won the match.

MURDO MACLEOD

Believe it or not, goals can change a game.

MICK CHANNON

To be a great game, one of the teams has to score first.

MARK LAWRENSON

Whelan was in the position he was, exactly.

JIMMY ARMFIELD

Football's football. If that weren't the case, it wouldn't be the game that it is.

GARTH CROOKS

It was one of those goals that's invariably a goal.

DENIS LAW

JOHN MOTSON: It's two—one to Italy with seventy minutes gone. If it remains like this for the next twenty minutes or so, how do you see it going, Terry?

TERRY VENABLES: Italy will go through.

Now both teams want the ball. Sheffield want the ball, and so do United.

CHRIS KAMARA

We are really the victims of our own problems.

JIMMY GREAVES

Apart from their goals, Norway wouldn't have scored.

TERRY VENABLES

The Croatians don't play well without the ball.

BARRY VENISON

I wouldn't be surprised if this game went all the
way to the finish.

IAN ST JOHN

Even if you tap it in from one yard it counts in the
record books as a goal, unlike the chances you miss.

JIMMY HILL

They only count when they go in the goal.

CHRIS KAMARA

It's different – it's not the same.

RYAN GIGGS

It was a game of two halves, literally.

CHRIS POWELL

It was easier to miss than score.

CLIVE ALLEN

You only get one opportunity of an England debut.

ALAN SHEARER

If England are going to win this match, they're going to have to score a goal.

JIMMY HILL

It's a no-win game for us. Although I suppose we can win by winning.

GARY DOHERTY

If you make the right decision, it's normally going to be the correct one.

DAVE BEASANT

Alan Shearer – two late goals, both in the last twenty minutes.

JON CHAMPION

To play Holland, you have to play the Dutch.

RUUD GULLIT

We lost because we didn't win.

RONALDO

There's no way the future's over for Martin Keown, Tony Adams or David Seaman.

ALAN SHEARER

The USA are a goal down, and if they don't get a goal they'll lose.

JOHN HELM

Leeds are enjoying more possession now that they have the ball.

SIMON BROTHERTON

The Italians are hoping for an Italian victory.

DAVID COLEMAN

I've always been a childhood Liverpool fan, even when I was a kid.

HARRY KEWELL

Bristol Rovers were four–nil up at half-time, with four goals in the first half.

TONY ADAMSON

You don't score sixty-four goals in eighty-six games without being able to score goals.

ALAN GREEN

If we played like this every week, we wouldn't be so inconsistent.

BRYAN ROBSON

Newcastle, of course, unbeaten in their last five wins.

BRIAN MOORE

I saw him kick the bucket over there, which suggests he's not going to be able to continue.

TREVOR BROOKING

What makes this game so delightful is that when both teams get the ball they're attacking their opponents' goal.

JIMMY HILL

A contract on a piece of paper, saying you want to leave, is like a piece of paper saying you want to leave.

JOHN HOLLINS

Scoring the first goal in soccer is very important, because your opponent is then faced with the task of having to score one to draw level and two to take the lead.

GRAHAM LEGGATT

If you're a goalkeeper, it doesn't matter what you save the ball with – if you keep it out, it's not a goal.

MARK LAWRENSON

You can't compare two players who are different because they're not the same.

GLENN HODDLE

It's a cup final, and the one who wins it goes through.

JIMMY HILL

John Bond has brought in a young left-sided midfield player, who, I guess, will play on the left side of midfield.

JIMMY ARMFIELD

And just to show you that great minds really do think alike . . .

If you want to win football games, you've got to score goals.

GRAHAM TAYLOR

If that had gone in, it would have been a goal.

DAVID COLEMAN

If that ball had crossed the line, it would have been a goal.

ANTONIO RATTIN

Sometimes in football you have to score goals.

THIERRY HENRY

If it had gone in, it would have been a goal.

BARRY DAVIES

If that had crossed the line it would have been a goal.

GARY BLOOM

No pain, no gain

Soccer can be a painful game. Strangely enough, it's the howlers concerning potentially painful antics that have us grimacing and laughing at the same time. Just be careful what you do with that frying pan. Oh, and take care where you put your groin . . .

Fortunately, Paul Scholes's injury wasn't as bad as we'd hoped for.

TREVOR BROOKING

Glenn is putting his head in the frying pan.

OSSIE ARDILES

We signed to play until the day we died, and we did.

JIMMY GREAVES

The groin's been a little sore, but after the semi-final I put it to the back of my head.

MICHAEL HUGHES

I felt a lump in my mouth as the ball went in.

TERRY VENABLES

If there are any managers out there with a bottomless pit, I'm sure that they would be interested in these two Russians.

DAVID PLEAT

Kevin Keegan has now tasted the other side of the fence.

DAVE MERRINGTON

The Scots have really got their hands cut out tonight.

TREVOR FRANCIS

Our guys are getting murdered twice a week.

ANDY ROXBURGH ON SOCCER'S HECTIC SCHEDULE

He was just about to pull the trigger on his left foot.

TERRY BUTCHER

He's looking around at himself.

JIMMY GREAVES

I took a whack on my left ankle, but something told me it was my right.

LEE HENDRIE

Craig Bellamy has literally been on fire.

ALLY McCOIST

Unfortunately, we keep kicking ourselves in the foot.

RAY WILKINS

In my day there were plenty of footballers around who would kick your b****cks off. The difference was that at the end they would shake your hand and help you look for them.

NAT LOFTHOUSE

Roy Keane, his face punches the air . . .

ALAN BRAZIL

Flo literally turned Taricco inside out.

TREVOR FRANCIS

That's often the best place to beat a goalkeeper, isn't it, between the legs?

CLIVE TYLDESLEY

Who's counting?

We thought we might have to abandon this category. How many entries is it possible to amass about arithmetically challenged footballers, after all? We still don't know how many there are, because we ran out of fingers.

With eight minutes left, the game could be won in the next five or ten minutes.

JIMMY ARMFIELD

The one thing England have got is spirit, resolve, grit and determination.

ALAN HANSEN

There's thirty minutes gone and we're in the first quarter of the game.

JON CHAMPION

I'm sure coach Frank Rijkaard will want the Dutch
to go on and score a fourth now – although
obviously they'll have to score the third one first.

ANGUS LOUGHRAN

Ritchie has now scored eleven goals, exactly double
the number he scored last season.

ALAN PARRY

I've had fourteen bookings this season – eight of which
were my fault, but seven of which were disputable.

PAUL GASCOIGNE

Unfortunately, we don't get a second chance. We've
already played them twice.

TREVOR BROOKING

Mirandinha will have more shots this afternoon
than both sides put together.

MALCOLM MACDONALD

If you had to name one particular person to blame, it
would have to be the players.

THEO FOLEY

So that's one–nil. Sounds like the score at Boundary Park, where of course it's two–all.

JACK WAINWRIGHT

If there's one thing Gus Uhlenbeek's got, it's pace and determination.

RAY HOUGHTON

Kilmarnock versus Partick Thistle, match postponed. That is, of course, a latest score.

FRANK BOUGH

I'm five short [of the Arsenal goal-scoring record] – not that I'm counting.

IAN WRIGHT

The first two-syllable word I learned when I was growing up was 'discretion'.

EAMONN DUNPHY

England are numerically outnumbered in the midfield.

MARK LAWRENSON

It's now one–one, an exact reversal of the scoreline on Saturday.

COMMENTATOR ON RADIO 5 LIVE

He has all-round, 365-degree vision.

ALAN MULLERY

Even if he had scored for Alaves, it would have made no difference to the scoreline.

GERRY ARMSTRONG

JIMMY HILL: Don't sit on the fence, Terry. What chance do you think Germany has got of getting through?

TERRY VENABLES: I think it's fifty–fifty.

He's only a foot away from the linesman – or should I say a metre, in modern parlance?

JIMMY ARMFIELD

They've one man to thank for that goal – Alan Shearer. And they've also got to thank referee Alan Wilkie.

CHRIS KAMARA

There's still forty-five minutes to go for both sides, I would guess.

BRIAN MARWOOD

I think you and the referee were in a minority of one, Billy.

JIMMY ARMFIELD

They're playing a four-four-one-one-one formation.

FRANK STAPLETON

He doesn't know how to spell the word 'give up'.

PAUL WADE

Both sides have scored a couple of goals, and both sides have conceded a couple of goals.

PETER WITHE

They'll perhaps finish in the top three. I can't see them finishing any higher.

DON HOWE

I don't think he's a thousand per cent mentally.

EAMONN DUNPHY

The World Cup is every four years, so it's going to be a perennial problem.

GARY LINEKER

The Bulgarian team are here with a relatively old squad. They impressed at USA '94, but, well, they're four years older now – most of them.

COMMENTATOR ON CBS

He had all the time in the world to kill a few seconds.

PAUL WADE

If England get a point, it will be a point gained as opposed to two points lost.

MARK LAWRENSON

Emmanuel Petit has won more medals than any other player in the Premiership this year, although Patrick Vieira's won the same medals.

BRIAN WOOLNOUGH

We were a little bit outnumbered there, it was two against two.

FRANK MCLINTOCK

Preki quite literally only has the one foot.

DAVID PLEAT

All the Leeds team are one hundred per cent behind the manager, but I can't speak for the rest of the squad.

BRIAN GREENHOFF

I think that France, Germany, Spain, Holland and England will join Brazil in the semi-finals.

PELÉ

I'd be surprised if all twenty-two players are on the field at the end of the game – one's already been sent off.

GEORGE BEST

When I said they'd scored two goals, of course I meant they'd scored one.

GEORGE HAMILTON

In the words of the old song, it's a long time from May to December but, you know, it's an equally long time from December to May.

JIMMY HILL

That was only a yard away from being an inch-perfect pass.

MURDO MACLEOD

Daei's all alone here, with four Chelsea defenders for company.

PETER DRURY

Neil Sullivan has stopped absolutely everything thrown at him: Wimbledon 1, Manchester United 1.

MIKE INGHAM

Four minutes to go . . . four long minutes . . . three hundred and sixty seconds . . .

ALISTAIR ALEXANDER

It's Denmark three, Denmark nil.

IAN BROWN

Ian Rush is deadly ten times out of ten, but that wasn't one of them.

PETER JONES

Fifty-two thousand here tonight, but it sounds like fifty thousand.

BRYON BUTLER

That youngster is playing well beyond his nineteen years – that's because he's twenty-one.

DAVID BEGG

Never go for a fifty–fifty ball unless you're eighty–twenty sure of winning it.

IAN DARKE

The only thing I have in common with George Best is that we come from the same place, play for the same club and were discovered by the same man.

NORMAN WHITESIDE

If you had a linesman on each side of the pitch in both halves you'd have nearly four.

ROBBIE EARLE

One year I played fifteen months.

FRANZ BECKENBAUER

We have one David Beckham playing abroad and that would be two.

JIMMY HILL

The one thing Gordon has brought to this team is a bit of work rate and team spirit.

ROBBIE EARLE

He was on the six-yard line, just two yards away from the goal.

PAT NEVIN

It was six and half a dozen, and six won.

CHRIS KAMARA

They're in pole position, i.e. third position, for the
Champions' League.

MARK LAWRENSON

There's going to be four or five teams battling for the
top six spots.

CHRIS WADDLE

One thing about Germany: they'll be organized,
they'll be big, and they'll be strong.

ALLY McCOIST

Eighty per cent of teams who score first in matches
go on to win them. But they may draw some.

DAVID PLEAT

That's down to one thing, fitness and organization.

NOEL KING

Peru score their third, and it's three—one to
Scotland.

DAVID COLEMAN

Body parts

Some of these, we admit, could have gone under 'Mixed-up metaphors', but so many howling good quotes from the world of soccer concern bits of the body, so we gave it a section to itself.

Let's close our eyes and see what happens.

JIMMY GREAVES

Zola's got two feet.

DAVID PLEAT

I've got a gut feeling in my stomach.

ALAN SUGAR

My left foot is not one of my best.

SAMMY McILROY

My legs sort of disappeared from nowhere.

CHRIS WADDLE

He's got a brain under his hair.

DAVID PLEAT

He's chanced his arm with his left foot.

TREVOR BROOKING

He held his head in his hands as it flashed past the post.

ALAN BRAZIL

Ian Rush unleashed his left foot and it hit the back of the net.

MIKE ENGLAND

England now have three fresh men, with three fresh legs.

JIMMY HILL

I think that their young legs would have found younger hearts inside them.

JIMMY ARMFIELD

RON ATKINSON: Unfortunately, it goes right down the goalkeeper's throat . . .

JOHN HELM: . . . where it hits him on the knees.

The left foot has helped – it's always been there, but I haven't always had the chance to use it.

STIG INGE BJORNEBYE

For such a small man, Maradona gets great elevation on his balls.

DAVID PLEAT

Left alone with our own heads on, we can be pretty mental.

TONY ADAMS

Martin Keown is up everybody's backsides.

TREVOR BROOKING

He's on the lips of every team in world football.

RAY HOUGHTON

Hagi has got a left foot like Brian Lara's bat.

DON HOWE

I was both surprised and delighted to take the armband for both legs.

GARY O'NEIL

Stoichkov is pointing at the bench with his eyes.

DAVID PLEAT

You're always going to be struggling if you haven't got a left foot.

TREVOR BROOKING

In the last ten minutes I was breathing out of my arse.

CLINTON MORRISON

Once Tony Daley opens his legs, you've got a problem.

HOWARD WILKINSON

He's one of those managers you'd give your left leg to play for.

COLIN COOPER

When Celtic get an opportunity to go above Rangers they've got to jump at it with both hands.

ALAN MULLERY

They've missed so many chances they must be wringing their heads in shame.

RON GREENWOOD

Hagi could open a tin of beans with his left foot.

RAY CLEMENCE

It seems that they're playing with one leg tied together.

KENNY SANSOM

He has two feet, which a lot of players don't have nowadays.

JIMMY HILL, REFERRING TO DAVID BECKHAM

They are breathing down the heels of Liverpool now.

GARY NEWBON ON MANCHESTER UNITED

Silvestre has had the whites of the goal in his eyes ever since.

IAN DARKE

And the bald head of John Sillett leaps from the
bench.

STUART LINNELL

He's one of those footballers whose brains are in his
head.

DEREK JOHNSTONE

Bobby Robson must be thinking of throwing some
fresh legs on.

KEVIN KEEGAN

Bruce, on his right foot, is still running.

ALAN GREEN

He signals to the bench with his groin.

MARK BRIGHT

Dumbarton player Steve McCahill has limped off
with a badly cut forehead.

TOM FERRIE

It's headed away by John Clark, using his head.

DEREK RAE

It's slightly alarming the way Manchester United
decapitated against Stuttgart.

MARK LAWRENSON

Celtic manager Davie Hay still has a fresh pair of
legs up his sleeve.

JOHN GREIG

He's got two great feet. Left foot, right foot, either side.

ALAN HANSEN

PSV have got a lot of pace up front. They're capable of exposing themselves.

BARRY VENISON

He's got a knock on his shin there, just above the knee.

FRANK STAPLETON

Simon Davies has had a few injuries. Maybe he wasn't fully foot.

TREVOR BROOKING

The fact that Burnley got beat here already will stick in their claw.

MARK LAWRENSON

Terry Venables has literally had his legs cut off from underneath him three times while he's been manager.

BARRY VENISON

Wayne Rooney really has a man's body on a teenager's head.

GEORGE GRAHAM

Time travel

You need the user's manual for the TARDIS to make temporal sense of some of these howlers.

He's got a great future ahead. He's missed so much of it.

TERRY VENABLES

As the seconds tick down, Belgium are literally playing in time that doesn't exist.

GUY MOWBRAY

He was in the right place at the right time, but he might have been elsewhere on a different afternoon.

TONY GUBBA

Dewalt had all kinds of time momentarily.

PAT MARSDEN

And Arsenal now have plenty of time to dictate the last few seconds.

DAVE BASSETT

He's started anticipating what's going to happen before it's even happened.

GRAEME LE SAUX

The time in the world has gotten shorter so it doesn't take so long to get to Australia.

PHIL NEAL

With eight or ten minutes to go, they were able to bring Nicky Butt back and give him fifteen to twenty minutes.

NIALL QUINN

I expect Chelsea to make a world-record signing in the near distant future.

TONY CASCARINO

There was three minutes to go about two minutes ago.

ALAN MULLERY

That was in the past – we're in the future now.

DAVID BECKHAM

Mixed-up metaphors

You don't need to keep your ears on the ball to see all kinds of problems surrounding the suspect use of metaphors. It's not just the mixed-up variety that we've found examples of, but also some wonderfully wacky similes, all of a sublimely surreal nature ...

We all know that promotion is the carrot at the end of the tunnel.

MARK YARDLEY

My team won't freeze in the white-hot atmosphere of Anfield.

RON SAUNDERS IN 1980 AS ASTON VILLA MANAGER

It's like a big Christmas pudding out there.

DON HOWE

She gives the players a shoulder to talk to.

NEIL WEBB ON EILEEN DREWERY,
FAITH HEALER USED BY GLENN HODDLE

Venison and Butcher are as brave as two peas in a pod.

JOHN SILLETT

This is a real cat-and-carrot situation.

DAVID PLEAT

A smoked-salmon sandwich of a football match if ever there's been one.

PETER DRURY

Sporting Lisbon in their green and white hoops, looking like a team of zebras.

PETER JONES

These managers all know their onions and cut their cloth accordingly.

MARK LAWRENSON

The Dutch look like a huge jar of marmalade.

BARRY DAVIES

In some respects, soccer's a bit like the dinosaur.
You give it a kick up the backside and three years
later its head drops off.

RON JONES

You must kill the bull or you haven't done nowt.

DANNY BERGARA, URUGUAYAN MANAGER OF
STOCKPORT IN 1992

For me, without exception, possibly my last World
Cup.

RAY WILKINS

There's a rat in the camp throwing a spanner in the
works.

CHRIS CATTLIN

That's understandable and I understand that.

TERRY VENABLES

I was really surprised when the FA knocked on my
doorbell.

MICHAEL OWEN

It slid away from his left boot, which was poised
with the trigger cocked.

BARRY DAVIES

Wembley is beginning to blacken with people in
terms of red and blue.

ALAN JACKSON

That's in the past, and the past has no future.

DAVID PLEAT

The beauty of cup football is that Jack always has a
chance of beating Goliath.

TERRY BUTCHER

What we have to do is put our teeth into the
Premiership.

PETER SCHMEICHEL

The eiderdown of this two–nil lead is a lot more comfortable than the blanket of one–nil.

GEORGE HAMILTON

The ball must be as slippery as a wet baby.

TONY GUBBA

St Mirren have been under the rack.

CHICK MURRAY

The Blackburn crowd have been saturated by fifty thousand Newcastle fans.

BRIAN LITTLE

Signori has all the tricks up his book.

RAY WILKINS

And there's Ray Clemence looking as cool as ever out in the cold.

JIMMY HILL

That would have been the icing on his start.

DAVID PLEAT

Madrid are like a rabbit dazed in the headlights of a car, except this rabbit has a suit of armour, in the shape of two precious away goals.

GEORGE HAMILTON

As you know, the result for City is not as bad as it sounds on paper.

STEVE MCILLWENN

The fans like to see Balde wear his shirt on his sleeve.

KENNY DALGLISH

That's bread and butter straight down the goalkeeper's throat.

ANDY GRAY

He hits it into the corner of the net as straight as a nut.

DAVID PLEAT

He's a two-legged tripod, if you know what I mean.

GRAHAM RICHARDS

The team must try to get their ship back on the road.

RAY WILKINS

The boss keeps those things up his sleeve, close to his chest.

CRAIG BURLEY

The club has literally exploded.

IAN WRIGHT

We defended like Trojans.

MIKE STOWELL

Now the world is my lobster.

KEITH O'NEILL

The championship is the carrot at the end of the championship.

TONY COTTEE

Manchester United have got the bull between the horns now.

BILLY MCNEIL

It's great to get the first trophy under the bag.

MICHAEL OWEN

The candle is still very much in the melting pot.

ALAN MCINALLY

The Arsenal defence is skating close to the wind.

JACK CHARLTON

The pace of the game between first team and
reserves is like night and day.

MAURICE MALPAS

He'll be the leader in the toolkit.

ROBBIE EARLE

The gelling period has just started to knit.

RAY WILKINS

All the cul-de-sacs are closed for Scotland.

JOE JORDAN

The tackles are coming in thick and thin.

ALAN BRAZIL

Liverpool have come out with all guns flying.

DENNIS TUEART

I can see the carrot at the end of the tunnel.

STUART PEARCE

It was a definite penalty but Wright made a right swansong of it.

JACK CHARLTON

Roy Keane didn't go through the book with a fine toothbrush.

TONY CASCARINO

And Swansea have an uphill mountain to climb now.

JOHN HARDY

As he was running away, the left back brought him down like a rabbit in full flight.

THIERRY ROLAND

They've come out with all cylinders flying.

LUTHER BLISSETT

From that moment the pendulum went into reverse . . .

GERALD SINSTADT

The crowd, a cacophony of colour.

PETER DRURY

Victor Hernandez, like an orchestral conductor directing his troops.

JON CHAMPION

A tale of too many cooks in the defence.

IAN BROWN

They're floating up on a sea of euphoria, and hoping to drag themselves clear of the quicksand at the bottom.

PETER JONES

Ian Baird is dashing around like a steamroller up front.

MARTIN TYLER

McCall is trying to thread a needle through a haystack there.

MARK BRIGHT

He was as game as a pebble.

DAVID WEBB

If ever the Greeks needed a Trojan horse, it is now.

GERALD SINSTADT

Poor Graham Shaw. It was there for the asking and he didn't give the answer.

PETER JONES

Like a predator about to devour the target.

ALAN PARRY

And Rush, quick as a needle.

RON JONES

In terms of the Richter scale this defeat was a force-eight gale.

JOHN LYALL

Celtic were at one time nine points ahead, but somewhere along the road, their ship went off the rails.

RICHARD PARK

Beckenbauer really has gambled all his eggs.

RON ATKINSON

The Uruguayans are losing no time in making a meal around the referee.

MIKE INGHAM

That was a needle-through-the-haystack job.

CLIVE ALLEN

He went down like a pack of cards.

CHRIS KAMARA

Peter Beardsley has got a few tricks up his book.

IAN SNODIN

Nobody took the responsibility of going to kill Yakin.

PAT BONNER

They think it's all over . . .

Well, this book is almost over. We'll bring this compilation to a close with a feast of a finale – a selection of quotable quotes that are guaranteed to keep you giggling long after the final whistle is blown.

The last player to score a hat-trick in a cup final was Stan Mortensen. He even had a final named after him – the Matthews final.

LAWRIE MCMENEMY

And now, *International Soccer Special*: Manchester United versus Southampton.

DAVID COLEMAN

I'd like to play for an Italian club, like Barcelona.

MARK DRAPER

There's no in between – you're either good or bad.
We were in between.

GARY LINEKER

What's the bottom line in adjectives?

PETER SHREEVES AFTER A HOME
LOSS TO COVENTRY IN 1985

I never predict anything, and I never will.

PAUL GASCOIGNE

I couldn't settle in Italy – it was like living in a
foreign country.

IAN RUSH

Footballers are the game's fodder, human sacrifices
that are thrown without sentiment or apologies into
the battlefield.

HUNTER DAVIES IN *A FOOTBALLER'S LOT*

Some people think football is a matter of life and
death. I assure you, it's much more serious than
that.

BILL SHANKLY

The road to ruin is paved with excuses.

BOBBY GOULD

Alcoholism v. Communism

BANNER AT A MATCH BETWEEN SCOTLAND
AND THE SOVIET UNION

All that remains is for a few dots and commas to be crossed.

MITCHELL THOMAS

Football hooligans? Well, there are ninety-two club chairmen for a start.

BRIAN CLOUGH

For me, it was a good match because I had a lot to do.

PETR CECH ON LETTING IN TWO GOALS,
LEADING TO HIS SIDE'S 2–0 DEFEAT

BARRY DAVIES'S BRAINWAVES

Cantona's expression – speaking the whole French dictionary without saying a word.

Poland nil, England nil, though England are now looking the better value for their nil.

A peep, peep, peep, another peep and that's it.

Nicky Butt, he's another aptly named player. He joins things, brings one sentence to an end, and starts another.

The crowd think that Todd handled the ball . . . they must have seen something that nobody else did.

That's lifted the crowd up into the air.

Lukic saved with his foot, which is all part of the goalkeeper's arm.

Martin O'Neill, standing, hands on hips, stroking his chin.

MIKE INGHAM

Jean Tigana has spent the entire first half inside Liam Brady's shorts.

JIMMY MAGEE

Ziege hits it high for Heskey, who isn't playing.

ALAN GREEN

That's the kind he usually knocks in in his sleep – with his eyes closed.

ARCHIE MACPHERSON

And now, the familiar sight of Liverpool raising the League Cup for the first time.

BRIAN MOORE

In England, soccer is a grey game played by grey people on grey days.

RODNEY MARSH

Football hooliganism is not a British disease. We simply perfected it.

LAURIE GRAHAM IN *THE BRITISH ABROAD*

I do love cricket – it's so very English.

SARAH BERNHARDT, WHO WAS WATCHING
A GAME OF FOOTBALL

Footeball . . . causeth fighting, brawling, contention, quarrel picking, murder, homicide and great effusion of bloode, as daily experience teacheth.

PHILIP STUBBES IN *ANATOMIE OF ABUSES*, 1585

He's showed him the left leg, then the right. Where's the ball? the defender asks. It's up his sleeve.

CLIVE TYLDESLEY

I always remember after a dull cup final at
Wembley, I was escorting the Queen to her car and I
said, 'Did you think anyone played well today,
ma'am?' and she said, 'Yes, the band.'

STANLEY ROUS, ON HIS TIME AS FA SECRETARY

Some of these players never dreamed they'd be
playing in a cup final at Wembley – but here they
are today, fulfilling those dreams.

LAWRIE MCMENEMY

He had to get down low to save that one on the
ground.

BARRY DAVIES

And then there was Johan Cruyff, who, at thirty-
five, has added a whole new meaning to the word
Anno Domini.

ARCHIE MACPHERSON

He's pulling him off! The Spanish manager is
pulling his captain off.

GEORGE HAMILTON

He went through a non-existent gap.

CLIVE TYLDESLEY

The substitutes are all on the bench, and that's
where they'll start the match.

BARRY DAVIES

Winning doesn't really matter as long as you win.

VINNY JONES

He's put on weight and I've lost it, and vice versa.

RONNIE WHELAN

He'd no alternative but to make a needless tackle.

PAUL ELLIOTT

The opening ceremony was good, although I missed it.

GRAEME LE SAUX

Ardiles strokes the ball like it was a part of his anatomy.

JIMMY MAGEE

He [Steve Walsh] is the type of player who will follow you to every end of the box.

KERRY DIXON

I'd rather play in front of a full house than an empty crowd.

JOHNNY GILES

Football's not like an electric light – you can't just flick the button and change from slow to quick.

JOHN GREIG

Sky.

GRAEME LE SAUX'S RESPONSE TO THE QUESTION:
WHICH IS YOUR FAVOURITE
COMMENTARY TEAM – BBC OR ITV?

I was disappointed to leave Spurs, but quite pleased that I did.

STEVE PERRYMAN

I spent four indifferent years at Goodison, but they were great years.

MARTIN HODGE

You've got to believe that you're going to win, and I believe that we'll win the World Cup until the final whistle blows and we're knocked out.

PETER SHILTON

TREVOR BROOKING'S BLOOPERS

That's football, Mike. Northern Ireland have had several chances and haven't scored, but England have had no chances and scored twice.

If you're going to score one goal or less, you're not going to get your victories.

It's end-to-end stuff, but from side to side.

He should have felt he probably scored then.

He's like an English equivalent of Teddy Sheringham.

Sometime in the ninety minutes they're going to have to win the game.

He looks as though he's been playing for England all his international career.

Well, I can play in the centre, on the right and occasionally on the left side.

DAVID BECKHAM'S ANSWER TO THE QUESTION: WOULD IT BE FAIR TO DESCRIBE YOU AS A VOLATILE PLAYER?

I'm not convinced that Scotland will play a typically English game.

GARETH SOUTHGATE

We didn't think we'd come here tonight and get any sort of result.

LES SEALEY

If there wasn't such a thing as football we'd all be frustrated footballers.

MICK LYONS

I can't promise anything, but I promise one hundred per cent.

PAUL POWER

I may have handed in a transfer request, but there is no way that I want to leave this club.

DAVID EYRES

Our consistency's been all over the place.

ANDY HINCHCLIFFE

I've lost count of the times I've played in that fixture. Each one was a memorable occasion.

TREVOR STEVEN

It was like the ref had a brand new yellow card and wanted to see if it worked.

RICHARD RUFUS

The manager has given us unbelievable belief.

PAUL MERSON

You don't need balls to play in a cup final.

STEVE CLARIDGE

Once you've had a bull terrier, you never want
another dog. I've got six bull terriers, a Rottweiler
and a bulldog.

JULIAN DICKS

I always used to put my right boot on first, and then
obviously my right sock.

BARRY VENISON

Without being too harsh on David Beckham, he cost
us the match.

IAN WRIGHT

If, since the start, I'd played well and put in some
good matches it would all have been too simple.

NICOLAS ANELKA

Historically, the host nations do well in Euro 2000.

TREVOR BROOKING

I can't even remember when the seventies was.

ROBBIE KEANE

I was born in Newcastle and I've played for
Newcastle Schoolboys all my life.

DENNIS TUEART

I've never wanted to leave. I'm here for the rest of
my life, and hopefully after that as well.

ALAN SHEARER

I dreamt of playing for a club like Manchester
United, and now here I am at Liverpool.

SANDER WESTERVELD

Leeds is a great club and it's been my home for
years, even though I live in Middlesbrough.

JONATHAN WOODGATE

I'm as happy as I can be – but I have been happier.

UGO EHIOGU

The ball went over mine and Colin Calderwood's heads and who should be there at the far post but yours truly – Alan Shearer.

COLIN HENDRY

I was alone up front, with Danny Murphy playing between me, myself and the midfield.

MICHAEL OWEN

In football, you don't really know what's going on, but we will worry about that when it happens.

NEIL SULLIVAN

The managerial vacancy at the club remains vacant.

TREVOR BROOKING

Maybe the mistakes have looked worse because they led to goals.

IAN WALKER

I find the growing intervention by the football authorities in strictly footballing matters a rather worrying trend.

KENNY CUNNINGHAM

I would not be bothered if we lost every game as long as we won the league.

MARK VIDUKA

If you don't believe you can win, there is no point in getting out of bed at the end of the day.

NEVILLE SOUTHALL

Alex Ferguson is the best manager I've ever had at this level. Well, he's the only manager I've actually had at this level. But he's the best manager I've ever had.

DAVID BECKHAM

One accusation you can't throw at me is that I've always done my best.

ALAN SHEARER

As a striker, you are either in a purple patch or struggling. At the moment, I'm somewhere in between.

BOB TAYLOR

It was like *déjà vu* all over again.

SHAKA HISLOP

I don't make predictions. I never have done and I never will do.

IAN WRIGHT

I faxed a transfer request to the club at the beginning of the week, but let me state that I don't want to leave Leicester.

STAN COLLYMORE

I definitely want Brooklyn to be christened, but I don't know into what religion yet.

DAVID BECKHAM

I was surprised, but I always say nothing surprises me in football.

LES FERDINAND

I was watching the Blackburn game on TV on Sunday when it flashed on the screen that George [Ndah] had scored in the first minute at Birmingham. My first reaction was to ring him up. Then I remembered he was out there playing.

ADE AKINBIYI

MARK LAWRENSON'S LORE

If Plan A fails, they could always revert to Plan A.

He can be as good as he wants to be, that's how good he can be.

Gary Neville was palpable for the second goal.

The number of chances they had before the goal they missed . . .

Michael Owen isn't the tallest of lads, but his height more than makes up for that.

It's like the Sea of Galilee: the two defenders just parted.

The longer the game went on, you got the feeling that neither side really wanted to lose.

They was given as good as they got.

JOHN TERRY

Ryan Giggs is running long up the back side.

RON ATKINSON

He's different, like every manager, I suppose.

UGO EHIOGU

I have a good record there. Played one, won one,
and hopefully it will be the same after Saturday.

STEVEN GERRARD

My parents have been there for me, ever since I was about seven.

DAVID BECKHAM

We have to be careful not to let our game not be the game we know it should be.

PAUL INCE

At least it was a victory and at least we won.

BOBBY MOORE

This is the one-off occasion and you can't get any bigger occasion than that.

BRYAN ROBSON

Everything in our favour was against us.

DANNY BLANCHFLOWER

That's a question mark everyone's asking.

BRUCE GROBBELAAR

We could be putting the hammer in Luton's coffin.

RAY WILKINS

You can only do as well as what you have done.

BRYAN ROBSON

Football's all about ninety minutes.

GLENN HODDLE

It feels like winning the cup final, if that's what it feels like.

GRAHAM HAWKINS

If you stand still there is only one way to go, and that's backwards.

PETER SHILTON

Wayne Rooney can go all the way to the top if he keeps his head firmly on the ground.

DAVID UNSWORTH

He managed to make a good hash of it in the end.

NIALL QUINN

I thought from start to finish we really started well.

JOHN HARTSON

The manager could not even talk to us at the
interval – he said we were bad.

JOHN TERRY

It's going to be difficult for me – I've never had to
learn a language and now I do.

DAVID BECKHAM

We seem to be a side that if we don't score we get
beat.

JASON MCATEER

It's not just the manager who makes the decision: it's
the player who makes the decision. They both
decide fifty–fifty to make a decision.

RUUD VAN NISTELROOY

Over the years a lot of great players have left United.
I'm sure the same will happen to me one day.

ROY KEANE

There won't be a dry house in the place.

MARK LAWRENSON

There's a smear campaign against me with facts
which are not true.

TONI POLSTER

Jörg Berger is such a good coach, he had even saved
the *Titanic*.

JAN AAGE FJORTOFT

When the seagulls follow the trawler it is because
they think sardines will be thrown into the sea.

ERIC CANTONA

Arguably, Blackburn have got the best forward line
in the Premiership. There's no denying that.

MARK LAWRENSON

We are now in the middle of the centre of the first
half.

DAVID PLEAT

The lad got overexcited when he saw the whites of
the goalpost's eyes.

STEVE COPPELL

The Saudis would struggle in Europe because of that problem with those prayers five times a day. You don't know if they're going to turn up for training. I'm being serious.

DON HOWE

They're still in the game, and they're trying to get back into it.

JIMMY HILL

BOBBY ROBSON'S RIDDLERS

I'd say he's the best in Europe, if you put me on the fence.

He's very fast and if he gets a yard ahead of himself nobody will catch him.

He never fails to hit the target, but that was a miss.

Ray Wilkins's day will come one night.

There will be a game where somebody scores more than Brazil and that might be the game that they lose.

Both teams – and Brazil, even – got better.

Manchester United will find it very intimidating with a hundred screaming fans in the Bernabeu.

Guppy has a dextrous left foot.

If you just came into the room and didn't know who was who, you'd obviously say Newcastle looked the most likely to score.

TERRY PAINE

A game is not won until it is lost.

DAVID PLEAT

Poor Miklosko. Hasn't had to make a save, yet he's let three goals in.

TREVOR FRANCIS

Tottenham have impressed me — they haven't thrown in the towel even though they have been under the gun.

BOBBY ROBSON

We're not used to weather in June in this country.

JIMMY HILL

He has a great understanding of where the goalkeeper is in relationship to the goal.

DAVID PLEAT

Brazil, the favourites, if they are the favourites, which they are . . .

BRIAN CLOUGH

They didn't change positions: they just moved the players around.

TERRY VENABLES

He's got perfect control over the ball right up to the minute he lets it go.

PETER WALKER

They're all on top of their game – fans and players alike.

DAVID FAIRCLOUGH

He'll be giving everything, but he hasn't got everything to give.

IAN ST JOHN

It's one of the greatest goals ever, but I'm surprised that people are talking about it being the goal of the season.

ANDY GRAY

There's no way that Ryan Giggs is another George Best – he's another Ryan Giggs.

DENIS LAW

He hit the post, and after the game people are going to say, 'Well, he hit the post.'

JIMMY GREAVES

It may have been going wide, but nevertheless it was a great shot on target.

TERRY VENABLES

Most of the players will be wearing rubbers tonight.

GARY LINEKER

It wasn't a bad performance, but you can't tell whether it was good or bad.

JIMMY HILL

The keeper was coming out in instalments.

JOE ROYLE

I'd like to see him scoring two or more goals in games which United win one–nil.

BRIAN WOOLNOUGH

Germany are probably, arguably, undisputed champions of Europe.

BRYAN HAMILTON

Fiorentina start the second half attacking their fans – just the way they like things.

RAY WILKINS

He is missing the absence of Dennis [Bergkamp].

BRIAN MARWOOD ON IAN WRIGHT

Manchester United have hit the ground running –
albeit with a three–nil defeat.

BOB WILSON

That's no remedy for success.

CHRIS WADDLE

ALAN MULLERY'S MUSINGS

To be fair, I don't think Les Ferdinand was fouled there – I think he went over on his own ability.

Well, I've seen some tackles, Jonathan, but that was the ultimatum!

. . . Jurgen Klinsmann, who refutes to earn £25,000 a week.

It doesn't endow me, to be honest.

I can't understand the notoriety of people.

Ipswich's pitch has been voted the best in the Premiership – in terms of surface, that is.

Bridge has done nothing wrong, but his movement's not great and his distribution's been poor.

Roy Evans bleeds red blood.

I don't want to be either partial or impartial.

FRANK McLINTOCK

Pires has got something about him – he can go both ways depending on who's facing him.

DAVID PLEAT

They've got their feet on the ground, and if they stay that way they will go places.

JOHN GIDMAN

He's like all great players – he's not a great player yet.

TREVOR FRANCIS

We're calling him the young player of the year, but he's only twenty years old.

ALAN MCINALLY

Dunfermline have a difficult month ahead over the coming two or three weeks.

DICK CAMPBELL

If Glenn Hoddle had been any other nationality, he would have had seventy or eighty caps for England.

JOHN BARNES

Kevin Keegan said if he had a blank sheet of paper, five names would be on it.

ALVIN MARTIN

He's not going to adhere himself to the fans.

ALAN MULLERY

The problems at Wimbledon seem to be that the club has suffered a loss of complacency.

JOE KINNEAR

They've been out a long time – credit them for getting back so quickly.

DAVID FAIRCLOUGH

It's his first cap, so he's not got a lot of experience at this level.

BRIAN MARWOOD

Oldham are leading 1–0, a well-deserved victory at this stage of the game.

TOMMY DOCHERTY

George will be happy with a draw – I know how ambitious and positive he is.

TERRY NEILL

He wasn't really trying to score with that shot.

DAVID PLEAT

Those are the sort of doors that get opened if you don't close them.

TERRY VENABLES

And tonight we have the added ingredient of Kenny Dalglish not being here.

MARTIN TYLER

And for those of you watching without television sets, live commentary is on Radio 2.

DAVID COLEMAN

Chris Waddle is off the pitch at the moment –
exactly the position he is at his most menacing.

GERALD SINSTADT

If they play together, you've got two of them.

DION DUBLIN

Romania are more Portuguese than German.

BARRY VENISON

Two–nil was a dangerous lead to have.

PETER BEARDSLEY

The ball could have gone anywhere and almost did.

BRIAN MARWOOD

The first half was end-to-end stuff. In contrast, in
this second half it's been one end to the other.

LOU MACARI

Barnsley have started off the way they mean to begin.

CHRIS KAMARA

He hasn't been the normal Paul Scholes today, and he's not the only one.

ALVIN MARTIN

Scotland don't have to score tonight, but they do have to win.

BILLY MCNEILL

. . . the Derby fans walking home absolutely silent in their cars.

ALAN BRAZIL

It's got nothing to do with his ability. In fact, it has got to do with his ability.

BARRY VENISON

That was an inch-perfect pass to no one.

RAY WILKINS

The front three are playing well in tandem.

ALAN MCINALLY

The difference between right and wrong is often not more than five metres.

JOHAN CRUYFF

There's Thierry Henry, exploding like the French train that he is.

DAVID PLEAT

Okon was booked for tackling Hamann's tackle.

DAVE BASSETT

I don't think anyone enjoyed it. Apart from the people who watched it.

ALAN HANSEN

When it comes to the David Beckhams of this world, this guy's up there with Roberto Carlos.

DUNCAN MCKENZIE

Gerry Taggart has been booked for a caution.

DAVE BASSETT

I don't think that record will ever be broken or beaten.

GERRY ARMSTRONG

He might play better if he shaves that beard.

CHARLIE NICHOLAS ON STEPHEN PRESSLEY

The midfield picks itself: Beckham, Scholes, Gerrard and A. N. Other.

PHIL NEAL

Paulo Wanchope has scored on sixty-seven minutes, and that's exactly the start Manchester City would have wanted.

DAVE BASSETT

Leeds have only had one shot on target, which may well have been the goal.

ANDY GRAY

I think Charlie George was one of Arsenal's all-time great players. A lot of people might not agree with that, but I personally do.

JIMMY GREAVES

They have more ability in the middle of the field in terms of ability.

JIMMY ARMFIELD

We have been saying this, both pre-season and before the season started.

LEN ASHURST

Yes, he's not unused to playing in midfield, but at the same time he's not used to playing there, either.

EMLYN HUGHES

Well, Terry, can you tell us where you are in the league, how far you are ahead of the second team?

IAN ST JOHN

That goal surprised most people, least of all myself.

GARTH CROOKS

It was a fair decision, the penalty, even though it was debatable whether it was inside or outside the box.

BOBBY CHARLTON

It was a good match, which could have gone either way and very nearly did.

JIM SHERWIN

He's perfectly fit, apart from his physical fitness.

MIKE ENGLAND

The only thing Norwich didn't get was the goal that they finally got.

JIMMY GREAVES

There are still hundreds of question marks to be answered.

JIMMY ARMFIELD

Walsall have given City more than one anxious moment amongst many anxious moments.

DENIS LAW

I'm afraid that Francis this season has been suffering from a panacea of injury.

DALE BARNES

They can crumble as easily as ice cream in this heat.

SAMMY NELSON

I'd like to have seen Tony Morley left on as a down-and-out winger.

JIMMY ARMFIELD

Whoever wins today will win the championship no matter who wins.

DENIS LAW

We sometimes think of Arsène Wenger as a general media population.

RODNEY MARSH

There are so many teams now down at the bottom of the Third Division. The FA really has to do something about it.

PETER LORIMER

He's the type of player the manager's either going to keep or not keep next season.

ALVIN MARTIN

It was one of those shots that just flew right along the floor.

JIMMY ARMFIELD

You could visibly hear the strain in his voice.

MIKE PARRY

The Belgians will play like their fellow Scandinavians, Denmark and Sweden.

ANDY TOWNSEND

A bit of retaliation there, though not actually on the same player.

FRANK STAPLETON

What would help the Ecuadorian side is if they could get a glimpse of the possibility of scoring a goal.

GRAHAM TAYLOR

Michael Owen is not a diver. He knows when to dive, and when not to.

STEVE HODGE

Once he's got confidence in his veins, he's a real threat.

ANDY TOWNSEND

The defenders did well, got their heads in, got their foots in.

EAMONN DUNPHY

I watched the game, and I saw an awful lot of it.

ANDY GRAY

From now on, it's the start of a new beginning.

DON GIVENS

One–all is probably a fair reflection of the score at half-time.

FRANK STAPLETON

You have to remember some of these guys are playing in front of the live cameras.

TONY GALE

You're not sure if the ball's going to bounce up or down.

FRANK STAPLETON

Solskjaer never misses the target. That time he hit the post.

PETER SCHMEICHEL

Djimi Traore had to adapt to the English game and he did that by going out on loan to Lens last season.

IAN RUSH

At the end of the day, the team with the most points are champions, apart from when it goes to goal difference.

TONY COTTEE

CHRIS KAMARA'S CRACKERS

Now they have got an extra yard of doubtness in their minds.

Statistics are there to be broken.

It really is an amazing result, nil–nil at half time.

. . . and it [the ball] just crept either side of the post.

It's real end-to-end stuff but, unfortunately, it's all up at Forest's end.

The atmosphere here is thick and fast.

For Burnley to win they are going to have to score.

Not only has he shown Junior Lewis the red card, but he's sent him off.

The Swedish back four is amongst the tallest in the World Cup. Their average age is seven foot four.

CHRIS WADDLE

He's good at that, David Beckham. He's good at kicking the ball.

JIMMY ARMFIELD

Even when he's changed the system from the four-three-three to the four-three-two, he's used the same players.

ADRIAN HEATH

It's what I call one of those 'indefensible ones' – you can't defend against them.

ANDY GRAY

He's hardly been on the pitch as many times as he's played.

ALVIN MARTIN

You certainly wouldn't bet against him not converting that chance.

BRIAN MARWOOD

It's his outstanding pace that stands out.

ROBBIE EARLE

ROB MCLEAN: John Hartson's playing superbly today.

SANDY CLARK: Yes, Rob, there's no one better today.

ROB MCLEAN: So, Sandy, who's your man of the match?

SANDY CLARK: Alan Thompson.

We have to remember Damien Duff is one of the most good players in the Premiership.

FRANK STAPLETON

I'm not going to pick out anyone in particular, but Jay Jay Okocha should not be the captain of a football club.

RODNEY MARSH

I think Arsenal will win the game, but I think Everton have a real good chance.

NIALL QUINN

They've forced them into a lot of unforced errors.

STEVE CLARIDGE

Derby County's chickens have literally come home to roost this season.

COLIN GIBSON

The goal that Charlton scored has aroused Arsenal.

GEORGE GRAHAM

Giggs came in from the left-hand right.

GEORGE BEST

The ball has broken fifty–fifty for Keegan.

DAVID COLEMAN

What will you do when you leave football, Jack –
will you stay in football?

STUART HALL

I would not say he's the best left-winger in the
Premiership, but there are none better.

RON AKTINSON ON DAVID GINOLA

An inch or two either side of the post and that would have been a goal.

DAVE BASSETT

What's it like being in Bethlehem, the place where Christmas began? I suppose it's like seeing Ian Wright at Arsenal.

BRUCE RIOCH

And I suppose they're nearer to being out of the FA Cup now than at any other time since the first half of this season, when they weren't ever in it anyway.

JOHN MOTSON ON SPURS

I think that was a moment of cool panic there.

RON ATKINSON

Tottenham are trying tonight to become the first London team to win this cup. The last team to do so was the 1973 Spurs side.

MIKE INGHAM

The game is balanced in Arsenal's favour.

JOHN MOTSON

You've got to miss them to score sometimes.

DAVE BASSETT

In comparison, there's no comparison.

RON GREENWOOD

I would also think that the action replay showed it to be worse than it actually was.

RON ATKINSON

Certain people are for me and certain people are pro me.

TERRY VENABLES

And I honestly believe we can go all the way to Wembley – unless somebody knocks us out.

DAVE BASSETT

I'm going to make a prediction – it could go either way.

RON ATKINSON

And with four minutes gone, the score is already nil–nil.

IAN DARKE

West Germany's Briegel hasn't been able to get past anyone yet – that's his trademark.

JOHN HELM

Both of the Villa scorers were born in Liverpool, as was the Villa manager, who was born in Birkenhead.

DAVID COLEMAN

What I said to them at half-time would be unprintable on the radio.

GERRY FRANCIS

Glenn Hoddle hasn't been the Hoddle we know. Neither has Bryan Robson.

RON GREENWOOD

I never comment on referees and I'm not going to break the habit of a lifetime for that prat.

RON ATKINSON

I don't think there is anybody bigger or smaller than Maradona.

KEVIN KEEGAN

The minute's silence was immaculate. I have never heard a minute's silence like that.

GLENN HODDLE

Welcome to Bologna on Capital Gold for England versus San Marino with Tennent's Pilsner, brewed with Czechoslovakian yeast for that extra Pilsner taste, and England are one down.

JONATHAN PEARCE

Lee Sharpe has got dynamite in his shorts.

STUART HALL

Referee Norlinger is outstanding in the sense that he stands out.

GEORGE HAMILTON

He's passing the ball like Idi Amin.

ALAN PARRY

What a debut for the young goalkeeper, as a striker.

PETER DRURY

One or two people are streaming away.

COMMENTATOR ON RADIO 5 LIVE

There are no opportune times for a penalty, and this is not one of those times.

JACK YOUNGBLOOD

This is the first time Denmark has ever reached the World Cup finals, so this is the most significant moment in Danish history.

JOHN HELM

The shot from Laws was precise, but wide.

ALAN PARRY

I predicted in August that Celtic would reach the final. On the eve of that final I stand by that prediction.

ARCHIE MACPHERSON

It's as if there's a magnet on the outside of the posts and bar.

JOHN HELM

. . . evoking memories, particularly of days gone by.

MIKE INGHAM

Forest have now lost six matches without winning.

DAVID COLEMAN

Such a positive move by Uruguay – bringing two players off and putting two players on.

JOHN HELM

McCarthy shakes his head in agreement with the referee.

MARTIN TYLER

Two–nil is a cricket score in Italy.

ALAN PARRY

Vialli's absolutely certain that he knows one way or the other whether he'll score or not.

JONATHAN PEARCE

The ageless Dennis Wise, now in his thirties . . .

MARTIN TYLER

He had a very impressive first debut.

COMMENTATOR ON GLR

He's thirty-one this year. Last year he was thirty.

DAVID COLEMAN

Ferguson hasn't scored since the opening day of the season – he's not a natural striker . . . Ferguson! At last a goal from him – natural instincts from a former Scottish striker.

ROB PALMER

The silence is getting louder.

DAVE WOODS

These Scottish players are very ordinary. In fact they have no names.

ZIMBABWEAN TV COMMENTATOR HAMMED ADIO

Kevin Reeves, proving an ill wind blows nobody no good.

DAVID COLEMAN

Lampard, as usual, arrived in the nick of time, but it wasn't quite soon enough.

ALAN PARRY

The fans, and now most of the crowd, are interested in this event.

ANGUS LOUGHRAN

It had to go in, but it didn't.

PETER DRURY

This will be their nineteenth consecutive game without a win unless they can get an equalizer.

ALAN GREEN

Viv Anderson has pissed a fatness test.

JOHN HELM

To a man, every Czech fan is on his or her feet.

GARY BLOOM

He had no chance of beating Schmeichel from there, but it was always worth a try.

ALAN PARRY

Every time they attacked, we were memorized by them.

CHARLIE NICHOLAS

Without the ball, he's a different player.

PETER BRACKLEY

The Baggio brothers, of course, are not related.

GEORGE HAMILTON

Xavier, who looks just like Zeus, not that I have any idea what Zeus looks like . . .

ALAN GREEN

It's just like they always say: too much too late.

TERRY BUTCHER

It's imperable [*sic*] that they get off to a good start.

CHARLIE NICHOLAS

A full-blooded encounter for a number of reasons, many of them illegitimate.

JON CHAMPION

Liverpool will be without Kvarme tonight – he's illegible.

JIMMY ARMFIELD

And he crosses the line with the ball almost mesmerically tied to his foot with a piece of string.

IAN DARKE

'Tempo' – now there's a big word.

BARRY VENISON

It's a renaissance – or, put more simply, some you win, some you lose.

DESMOND LYNAM

They get to about thirty yards out and then everything goes square and a bit pedantic.

CHARLIE NICHOLAS

It's a tense time for managers. They have to exhume confidence.

GARY LINEKER

Football's a game of skill: we kicked them a bit and they kicked us a bit.

GRAHAM ROBERTS

All Michael O'Mara titles are available by post from:

Bookpost, PO Box 29, Douglas, Isle of Man IM99 1BQ

Credit cards accepted.
Telephone: 01624 677237
Fax: 01624 670923
Email: bookshop@enterprise.net
Internet: www.bookpost.co.uk

Free postage and packing in the UK.

Other Michael O'Mara Humour titles:

All Men Are Bastards – ISBN 1-85479-387-X pb £3.99
The Book of Urban Legends – ISBN 1-85479-932-0 pb £3.99
Born for the Job – ISBN 1-84317-099-X pb £5.99
The Complete Book of Farting – ISBN 1-85479-440-X pb £4.99
Complete Crap – ISBN 1-85479-313-6 pb £3.99
The Ultimate Book of Farting – ISBN 1-85479-596-1 hb £5.99
The Ultimate Insult – ISBN 1-85479-288-1 pb £5.99
Wicked Cockney Rhyming Slang – ISBN 1-85479-386-1 pb £3.99
Wicked Geordie English – ISBN 1-85479-342-X pb £3.99
Wicked Scouse English – ISBN 1-84317-006-X pb £3.99
The Wicked Wit of Jane Austen – ISBN 1-85479-652-6 hb £9.99
The Wicked Wit of Winston Churchill – ISBN 1-85479-529-5 hb £9.99
The Wicked Wit of Oscar Wilde – ISBN 1-85479-542-2 hb £9.99
The World's Stupidest Criminals – ISBN 1-85479-879-0 pb £3.99
The World's Stupidest Graffiti – ISBN 1-85479-876-6 pb £3.99
The World's Stupidest Laws – ISBN 1-85479-549-X pb £3.99
The World's Stupidest Men – ISBN 1-85479-508-2 pb £3.99
The World's Stupidest Signs – ISBN 1-85479-555-4 pb £3.99
More of the World's Stupidest Signs – ISBN 1-84317-032-9 pb £4.99
The World's Stupidest Last Words – ISBN 1-84317-021-3 pb £4.99
The World's Stupidest Inventions – ISBN 1-84317-036-1 pb £5.99
The World's Stupidest Instructions – ISBN 1-84317-078-7 pb £4.99
The World's Stupidest Sporting Screw-Ups – ISBN 1-84317-039-6 pb £4.99
Shite's Unoriginal Miscellany – ISBN 1-84317-064-7 hb £9.99
Cricket: It's A Funny Old Game – ISBN 1-84317-090-6 pb £4.99